# This book is written to help understanding that there is another way in which we can live our lives and to give a greater understanding of our existence, on this little blue planet that we affectionately call home.

**We are only here for a blink of an eye, so enjoy your time here.**

I would like to state that although this book mentions God, hope and faith, that it is not a religious book in anyway, but that does not mean to offend any cultures or their beliefs in god, but rather the term is used as a universal language to the word God.

All the information retained in this book is gathered through resources: Google search and links through You-tube. The information is a guide and its recommended that people source other related works in the field of self help. All information is for research purposes and by using the information will not guarantee success if not used as explained in the relevant information.

Every one who reads and undertakes the practices of this research, will find results will be varied upon the application and use of the supplied information. Knowledge is not power power is putting that knowledge into action. obtaining power and knowledge from these resources supplied and by searching other reading material will go along way to obtaining you objective. That being said the information that is available in this book and the research that you have links to EG: Think and Grow Rich, Earl Nightingales The Strangers Secret, Bob Proctor videos, and other useful resources, have helped countless people transform their lives and become financially independent. Napoleon Hills book Think and Grow Rich Has helped thousands and sold over millions of copy's world wide.

 The Author of this book has given you the opportunity to use resources that are readily available through searching through Google Search and YouTube videos.

The personal Story's of the Author are used as a reference for the reader to understanding how using these resources have help you and countless others transform their lives and help obtain a positive mental attitude towards humanity and the zest to live on this blue planet.

The author also would like to add at the time of publishing this book that these service that he has offered in forms of links and YouTube videos were available for viewing at the time of writing this book and that he has no control if these resources are no longer active.

**60 years Gone**
**By Stephen Bowker**

**Written April 2022**

## CONTENT

# Forward

Purchasing this book tells me you are a wake, believe me there are a lot out there who are not and it tells me you are ready to change your life. One of the hardest decisions in someones life is to realise that its time for change and I applaud you for taking that step.

Change is like stepping out of your comfort zone, its hard its going into the fear not knowing if you will make the grade. And your right to have that fear as Earl Nightingales explains in "The Strangers Secret" He tells us that of the 100 people who try to become financial independent 5 get to the finishing line and become financially independent. Only 1 out of that 5 becomes rich. So to take the first step which is where you are now, puts you in the 100%

When I did my film course and I found this with other thing in my life that I did courses for was that the class will start on day one with twenty students by day seven down to eight students then by the end of the course two weeks later you have a class of six. This comes down to people not ready to leave their comfort zone, some refer to it as the fear barrier. They are just not prepared to take that leap, to take make that change.

The first step is the hardest. This statement is so true and people fail to take that first step because of fear of the unknown and secondly fear of criticism, people are worried about what their family, friends or work will say.

Let me ask you a question and just give me a yes or no answer,
If I said leave your job today and spend two years working for me without any pay or financial support whats so ever from me, told you that you had to spend ever waking hour working on a project, meaning no time for family and friends, then I told you that at the end of that two year you would have endless riches. What would be your answer?

Ponder that.

Well that is exactly what Napoleon Hill was asked, but when Andrew Carnegie the richest man in the world in 1930 said to Napoleon he had an assignment that would take no less than 20 years and he would receive no payment from him and Nepolean had to pay his own way. Well Napoleon did not know Carnegie had a stop watch under the desk and Napoleon to get the assignment he had 30 seconds to make that decision. And Nepolean told Carnegie in less than 25 seconds that he would take the job. Napoleon was assigned to find out from the most successful people in the world what counts for success. In other words what was the secret that made men rich and financially successful. The book Napoleon Hill spent 20 years researching was called Think and Grow Rich. Before Napoleons death in 1970 Think and Grow rich had sold countless million of copy's. Napoleon Hill took the job in 1936 he had but a few dollars in his pocket, in no way when he took that assignment was he well off, in fact days before taking the assignment he had told his younger brother that he would help him get the money to go to collage. Nepolean had to tell his brother he had taken a job in which he would receive no money for 20 years. In 1970 when Napoleon died he was a millionaire.

By applying the principle that I am sharing in this book, several thousand men and women have see riches and it has changed their life's, some came from poverty stricken conditions. The principles I am sharing in this book has made countless millionaires around the world, even our great leaders and our forefathers used these principles when signing the deceleration of independence and changed the world.

For the people that are prepared to put it all on the line have no recourse but to follow through, are the ones that win and become that 5%  Will you be in that 5%?

Your mind set and attitude is what will set you up for financial freedom.
I am reminded of a story I was told when working for an insurance company in Perth around 200. We sold accident insurance at the time, The story was in the 1970s two top shoe salesmen in New York were called into their bosses office, he had a job for them. After about 30 minutes the two men left the office one of the salesmen looked like he had been given some horrific news and the other one was deliriously excited. Well a colleague approached the salesman with the long face and asked what was wrong, the salesman grudgingly replied "They are sending us to Tanzania in South Africa to set up a shop and sell shoes, nobody in South Africa wears shoes."  The sales man looked at the other salesman who was laughing and so excited, he said "Why are you so happy"? The sales man said with such enthusiasm "This is great nobody in Tanzania has shoes we will sell an abundance every day.

The difference with these two salesman is attitudes, one looked at it with doom a dread the other with optimism and an opportunity.

What you will find throughout this book is how opening the mind and having a great attitude can change the way you perceive any given situation.

My hope is that many who read this book will go on to find their success and financial freedom. You will understanding what a beautiful opportunity we have been given to be hear and to do what we were born to do to **create.**

Share this knowledge with everyone you can and we can all live with love joy and abundance.

# What happened to my life?

You wake up one morning and you realise time has past you by. As you look back you say "What happened, were did my life go"?

Well I can not answer that question for you, but I do know, that I spent my life wondering who I was and spend sixty years, before I woke up and said "What happened to my life

Are We Hard Wired That Way?

They say we live the life we are programmed to live. The masses believe that we are born and learn the basics from our parents, Although some have a great start others don't get that great a start and their life spirals out of control, what we refer to as a bum deal.

Let me Ask you, are you one of five, or eight maybe ten siblings? or were you an only child.? It doesn't really mater because we are all brought up with the same rules in the house, and at school, we reform to those rules and conditions.

Take My neighbour Mary she was eight years old she had two younger brothers and a younger sister, This was around 1968. I was 8 and lived at home with my 5 older brothers two older sisters and my little sister. Mary and her brother Robert were very bright students top of the class you could say, if the teacher asked the class a question on maths English or any subject we had studied, Mary's hand shot up tall and proud, you could see her busting to be picked to answer from the foray of hands that were held up, My hand never went up, I could never considerate, no I was not ADHD, (attention-deficit hyperactivity disorder.) Was that even a thing in the 60s? My mind just wondered constantly about being anywhere but there.

Back in them days my older sister and brother walked us home from school, we lived but 4 blocks from the school around a fifteen minute walk, if I didn't dawdle along. My sister was constantly yelling at me "Stephen move" as she shunted me forward to keep me moving.

Once home there was no stopping me, I would race off to play. Now Mary and her brother as far as I know never walked to school, so I assumed their mother picked them up. Not that I noticed or cared either way. What I did notice, was that why me and my sister played out the back we never sore Mary and her brothers playing in their yard after school, well I may not have cared about much but I was inquisitive, One day at lunch time I asked Robert why I never see them playing in their yard after school or on weekends. I was stunned at his reply. Robert placed his sandwich on the brown wrapping his mother used to wrap his lunch in, I noticed this because my lunch was wrapped in a newspaper my dad had read the night before. Robert then looked up at me and said "My mother is a teacher When we get home we are home schooled for two hours then do our choirs we have our bath eat our dinner and bed," He them picked up his sandwich and started eating. I although ok and ran off to the oval to play.

Fast forward to 15 years Mary became a chemist Robert became a surgeon and the other two worked in high paying jobs. Me I was unemployed still trying to figure out what I wanted to do, and I did at 34, I realised I wanted to be a lawyer. I found out I was looking at a good two years of schooling, I had to do year 11 and 12 that I did not complete, then I was looking at five years of law study at a university. Remembering how much I hated school I said pass. I did do a year off accounting then pulled out, again it got to hard so I quite, I told myself I cant do it, that I hated it and every day it became harder and harder and every day I said I cant do this. I was training my subconscious mind to fail, but I did pass year 11 legal study's.

Going back to Mary and her family, I always wondered, did they succeed because their mum made them do home schooling 7 days a week for 10 years of their school life? Or did they do it because they wanted a better life? I did get the answer.

My old primary school held a celebration for the kids who finished year 7 (this was in the eights) a heap of us were invited to go along, well I bumped into Mary and she looked nothing like the little girl with glasses she was quite stunning very well dressed. I was not, I heard it was fancy dress so I went dressed as Fred Flinstone and my costume was a potato sack turned up side down with a whole for my head and my arms and I had shorts on of course, unbeknown to me the dress up was for the kids. I looked ridiculous and there I stood in front of Mary. Well once she stopped laughing and that took a while, she would stop look at me and start again, I just stood there. it was then I asked what she was doing and she asked what work I was in. Mary told me she was a head chemist making around hundred thousand a year and what her brothers and younger sister was doing and that Robert was a surgeon. I smiled and she asked what i do, being em-barest I said i am waiting for the right opportunity to come along and I was doing well. She smiled not sure what to make of that, so I asked her the question I had been thinking about, "Did you and your family do well because you had home schooling from you mum"? This question threw her a little, and she was startled by the beach ball that came hurtling our way. I managed to catch it and throw it back to the children. She looked at me and said "What my my mother did for us was great, ok we didn't get to play and be out with friends after school and on weekends and because of that my life is great and now I have the time and money to go away on holidays and get a nice car and have fun, plus I love what I do every day." She then stopped and looked at me. "Stephen I didn't do what I did because I was home schooled, I did what I did to make my mum proud of what i have achieved and mum loved teaching, she was able to follow her passion by teaching us."

Now to many that was a learning moment. If I had of cared about the answer. I just wanted to know so nothing sank in, I smiled and said "Oh look their is mickey" and moved off.

The lesson here is I was still not ready, I had no goals no direction, Mary could have given me a formula to be filthy rich that night but I wouldn't have seen it, because I was not ready for it.

## The Author

Let me introduce myself, my name is Stephen Bowker I am 60 years old and have just woke up, yes like hundreds of thousands of people I have been a sleep a zombie, just following the masses and going nowhere. I started my life as a furniture removal man, at 15. I left school half way through year 9, in Australia that is first year of highs school. From there I moved into other labour jobs, married at 18 divorced with two children at 23. Being hit hard by the breakup my life spiralled out of control. I couldn't hold a job had no idea what or were my life was headed and it was like that the rest of my life booze and recreational drugs.

I guess mixing with the wrong people in my life, it did not get any better, its now that I am in my sixty's that I say what happened were did my life go. I often think about Mary and find myself saying well done Mary, Mary who knew at an early age what she wanted and went for it. If only I had of listened more, learnt that education and knowledge matter then I too could have had a prosperous life like Mary.

If we all look around the signs are there we just have to open our eyes and our minds. Through out this book I am going to wake up your conscious mind and you will be astonished how powerful you are. Within this book you will be given quotes from some of the richest people in the world, gone now some, but still there are still some here.

This will only help you if you are willing to believe in you, yes believe in your ability to change and do what you want to do, this is not a get rich quick book, I am **not** a Guru nor am I an entrepreneur. I am a regular Joe like you, teaching something that has change my beliefs and made me see, that we are truly special, we are capable of enjoying the abundance that awaits us.

Note being successful doesn't mean being rich it means being educated having the knowledge, if you learn anything in this book, learn that knowledge is important, knowledge will help you understanding that we can achieve anything we desire. Knowledge is not power action is power if you put your ideas a thoughts into action then that is powerful.

There is no costs or sales ploy, all we ask is for your time and belief, that's it.

I will be straight with you, you don't get nothing for nothing, you have to be prepared to put in the time and effort to get the life you want. I know you have heard it all before you have payed out money after money and still today looking for the answer.

Depending on what you want to do, maybe its get that promotion or a pay rise, it could be to finally afford that new car or get that a new job or financial freedom.

I have a question for you and if you answer is yes then this book is for you.

Can you imagine? Can you open your mind and dream? Do you have a dream? Whats your dream/ What are you prepared to do to see your dream manifest it self? Are you ready to change your life?

If you want to change your life, lose weight, get that great partner, run your own business, what ever it is Are you ready to achieve it?

If your answer was Yes then welcome aboard.

This book will show you that you are capable of getting everything you want all you have to do is say out load

Yes i am Willing to change my life
Yes I am Ready to change my life

Yes I am Able to change my life.

Say it Again.

Yes i am Willing to change my life
Yes I am Ready to change my life
Yes I am Able to change my life.

## I cant hear you, louder

Yes i am Willing to change my life
Yes I am Ready to change my life
Yes I am Able to change my life.

Now you are ready to change your life.

## You can change your life you can have anything you want.

We tend to gravitate to books were the writers have gone from rages to riches and listening to their story's and find the secret. I am not going to tell you I was broke I struggled through life to make millions of dollars, because to be honest who wants to hear how some one says "ten years ago I was broke now I have millions a new Lamborghini five houses in Florida and a jet that I use to take the family on holidays when ever we want." Who wants to hear that? You may be struggling trying to change your life for yourself, your family. You want to know how to get financially independent or how to loose those pounds or how to start your successful business. If a guru is flashing money and cars and million dollar houses and boats then wants you to pay for the system and funnel to make you a millions, Run yes run because if they have millions why do they need your money?

What you will not hear is some guru offering you the world or screaming pay now. What you will hear is how people like Napoleon Hill was given a job that took him twenty years to research.

By the way what was your answered I ask at the opening of this book was it yes no to working for 2 years for no pay?

Today I still don't know what I would have said to Andrew Carnegie.

You will hear from Earl Nightingale and Bob Proctor and many other entrepreneurs who were exactly where you are today and turned their life around and lived a life of joy, love and abundance, all because they took action, they followed the advise from people who made changes in their lives and took control. The other thing they did was they had a mentor someone they looked up to some on they admired and aspired to be like if I was truthfully honest, I would say in many ways Bob Proctor was my mentor even though we never met. I listened to his videos I followed his advise. Bob Proctor new where his life was headed I was following him not the masses.

You will understanding how you already have greatness in you and all it takes is for you to listen and implement the steps to become who ever you want and have the life and freedom you deserve. And all it cost you is Time, your time and the ability to dream.

## Does it work?

Andrew Carnegie made thousands of men rich and financial independent. Napoleon Hill made hundreds of thousands richer and financially independent with this formula. Does it work? Try it and see for yourself.

There is something I need you to understanding before you read on.

The principles in this book are talking about the mind and what you need to understanding is for you to benefit you have to reprogram your thinking. You have to be prepared to put in the time and commitment to make changes to your life, this is were we lose a lot of the 100% at the being of this transformation its hard, don't kid yourself this will be one of the hardest things you have ever done, saying that if you are committed to change and I mean really committed, you are over the day to day you are over scraping to get by, over watching everyone else have what you are longing for, then you have to be prepared to put in the time.

Are you prepared to put in the time to change the course of your like            Yes
Are you prepared to spend three months listening to the material over and over every day   Yes
Are you prepared to open your mind and listen to your thoughts            Yes
Are you prepared to dream            Yes
Are you prepared to set goals            Yes
Are you prepared to write out you goals and read them aloud every day            Yes
Are you prepared to take a way time from family and friends to achieve your goals            Yes
Are you prepared to meditate twice a day            Yes
Are you prepared to handle criticism from family and friends            Yes
Are you prepared to except winners never quit            Yes
Are you prepared to sacrifice your time to give you and you family a better life            Yes
Are you prepared to rid yourself of hatred, envy, Jealousy, Selfishness and cynicism            Yes
Are you prepared to develop love and joy for all humanity            Yes
Are you prepared to develop and maintain a positive mental attitude            Yes

If you can answer yes to all of these you are well on your way to the top 5%

## People around the world are waking up

One day you wake up and you say were did it go? That seams to be happening world wide people are waking up and wondering why it took them so long to see whats been right in front of them all their lives. Explaining this concept can sometimes be hard, I think Bob Bob Proctor explains this well here. But don't just watch the clip do what he tells you and you will see how quickly your life will start to change.

Copy link and add to your task bar to watch.

https://youtu.be/Vkb4ZgHYoXw

How to Improve Your Self Image with Bob Proctor on YouTube.

This clip it will help you understanding the workings of the mind, if you want to change your life don't dismiss this. Every journey has a beginning a middle and an end. For you to understanding the beginning of your journey it starts here.

As stated earlier in the book you must be able to open your mind and believe in yourself. When the Wright brothers believed in their goal they changed the world as did Carl Benz. Remember I did say it was going to take work and dedication. This is to help you grow, take your life back, many will tell you your crazy even some will say brainwashed. They are the ones struggling working 12 hour days for minimum wage and living check to check so you have to decide what life you want to live. Listen to your friends who are struggling day to day or listen to people who have lived that life and found a better smarter way to live, giving you your life back and time with your family. Remember only you can decide.

Emerson decided he was going to follow his dream and now we have light to see in the dark what would have happened if he listened to his family and friends? Who more than likely told him he was a fool and a dreamer.

There are very few people alive who have invested more time studying success than Bob Proctor. He has spent almost all day, every day, for thirty-three years analysing success. Over the years, he has had many failures, but has also had numerous exciting wins on many continents around the world with millions of dollars involved. The wins and the failures have both proven to be extraordinary personal learning experiences.

These are the core lessons that Bob has learned and mastered throughout his illustrious career of dedicated study, rigorous application, trial and error, and, of course, BIG wins.

When it comes to systematising life, no one else can touch him. He is simply the best.

Let Bob lead you through his 12 principles for finding success. Instantly apply them to your own life. It will begin to impact you long before your reach the last chapter. Let Bob teach you about:

- •CONFIDENCE
- •PERSISTENCE
- •GOALS
- •SUCCESS
- •ATTITUDE
- •COMMUNICATION
- •ACTION
- •DECISION
- •RISK
- •RESPONSIBILITY

- •MONEY
- •CREATIVITY

There are a few people who are truly successful and many others who work hard all of their lives attempting to be successful. As a result, the average person believes that success is hard to obtain and that those who do achieve it are either lucky or extremely brilliant.

Most people are so busy attempting to make ends meet that they never take the time to really study the highly successful people. Every person who has made such a study has arrived at the same shocking conclusion: success is merely a decision. You must decide what you want and then begin moving toward it. You decide where you are, and you begin with whatever you have. That's it.

*"The only limits in our life are those that we impose on ourselves."*

-BOB PROCTOR

Sometime we have to walk in someone else shoes before we understanding the path we must walk. By learning from those who have to pound the payment and cleared the path so you can enter with the knowledge needed, is like having that Jeannie in the bottle. Just remember not all roads are paved with gold but follow Bob i am pretty sure they are leading you to your destination of prosperity and financial success.

Bob Was quick to point out if you see a mass of people heading in one direction and one lonely sole heading the opposite detection, follow that sole as he knows were hes going.

To often we get court up in the confusion going on around us and its easy to follow others without thinking "Were are they going"? It takes but a moment to stop and look at whats happening around you. Once in a while look up and see your world and all its splendour, in stead of a screen that is made to distract you.

Next time you get on a train or bus put your phone in your pocket and enjoy the ride. Look at the buildings and roads and houses and trees and signs and think "wow all this was once a though in some ones mind "and Yes the tree, someone thought to plant it there, enjoy what you have out there. Get off your devise for 20 to 30 minutes and let you mind wonder and maybe you will find that next great idea.

The other great thing with putting your phone away you now see real people, try this today. Smile at someone and I guarantee he or she will smile back and you might have just brightened up their day. No one knows whats going on in other peoples lives and that smile could be what they needed to kick start their day. They may even smile at someone else making that persons day. Who knows how many people your one mile could help that day. And it cost nothing to smile but its worth a lot to someone.

## Laughter is Therapeutic

The other day I was laying on my bed just answering messages and something popped in my mind, i am not sure if you have seen the yellow pages add "Not happy Jan" if you haven't google it, anyway something happened earlier that day a client cancelled and it annoyed me a bit and it was on my mind, Well that add popped into my head and I could see myself opening the window and yelling "Not happy Jan" and the client is running off, well I could see this in my mind and I started laughing for a moment then I stopped, then suddenly I start laughing again this time longer it got to the stage every time I stopped I started laughing again now I was in tears of laughter and I mean it was a belly laugh. I am so glad my phone didn't ring because there was no way I could stop laughing long enough to answer it. Well eventually I did stop and for the next three hours I was in the best mood, now I had not laughed like that for over has to be 15 years but it felt so good just to laugh over a little thing. So next time you get upset over something let your Jan out and have a roaring laugh and watch your day change from misery to happiness.

We have the ability to change the way we feel, all we have to do is stop and see how that thing looks when you put it in a funny moment.

## The Strangest Secret- by Earl Nightingale

Do you know what will happen to 100 individuals who start even at the age of 25, and who believe they will be successful? By the age of 65, only five out of 100 will make the grade! Why do so many fail? What happened to the sparkle that was there when they were 25? What became of their dreams, their hopes, their plans...and why is there such a large disparity between what theses people intended to do and what they actually accomplished? That is... The Strangest Secret. Some years ago, the late Nobel prize-winning Dr. Albert Schweitzer was asked by a reporter, "Doctor, what's wrong with men today?; The great doctor was silent a moment, and then he said, "Men simply don't think!" It's about this that I want to talk with you. We live today in a golden age. This is an era that humanity has looked forward to, dreamed of, and worked toward for thousands of years. We live in the richest era that ever existed on the face of the earth... a land of abundant opportunity for everyone.

the hopes, the plans... and why is there such a large disparity between what these people intended to do and what they actually accomplished?

University students with qualifications coming out the end of their business cards,

It seams to be a trend in this century at least that people are not waking up until they have lived half their life and then say what did I do with my life.. Its been said that the education system doesn't help.

**Bob Proctor stated "people are coming out of university with qualifications coming out the end of their business cards."**

but they are not getting jobs or their taking medium low paid jobs. So whats the answer?

Many will say it cant be changed the system is in place, others will say the system is broken. In fact its not broken it just needs to change, its amazing how science who was all out of wack with faith and hope and things they cant see, but now even they understanding the laws of vibration, and now understanding that faith hope and belief are now an excepted theory. (only took like 150 so years) This now can change our education system, to see that you can think outside the box, you can do what ever your mind conceives.

"If you can see it in your mind you can holds it in your hand."

**Think and Grow Rich Nepleon Hill.**

In the late 1990s I was told about Think and Grow Rich and a book called Chicken Soup for the Sole by Jack Canfield. After hearing the names of the books and I was not much of a reader except for crime novels I Passed. It was not until Think and Grow Rich was an audio tape that I resonantly came across that I listened to it and I now wish I had of had this book when I was in my twenty's. Not that it would have made a difference as I stated earlier in the book with Mary, I was not ready for it.

I listen to the 4 recording every day now and I pick up something new every day. As for Chicken Soup for the Soul, I still haven't read it, that doesn't mean you shouldn't.

Along with Earl Nightingale I got a lot from these recording and can highly recommend you have a listen thereby create a life of frustration, fear, anxiety and worry. And if he thinks about nothing … he becomes nothing.

### AS YE SOW and SO SHALLYE REAP

The human mind is much like a farmer's land. The land gives the farmer a choice. He may plant in that land whatever he chooses. The land doesn't care what is planted. It's up to the farmer to make the decision. The mind, like the land, will return what you plant, but it doesn't care what you plant. If the farmer plants two seeds, one a seed of corn, the other nightshade, a deadly poison, waters and takes care of the land, what will happen?

Remember, the land doesn't care. It will return poison in just as wonderful abundance as it will corn. So, up come the two plants and one corn, one poison as it's written in the Bible, "**As ye sow, so shall ye reap.**"

The human mind is far more fertile, far more incredible and mysterious than the land, but it works the same way. It doesn't care what we plant. **SUCCESS** or **FAILURE**. *A concrete, worthwhile Goal or Confusion, Misunderstanding, Fear, Anxiety, and so on*. But what we plant it must return to us.

The problem is that our mind comes as standard equipment at birth. It's free. And things that are given to us for nothing, we place little value on. Things that we pay money for, we value.

Copy and add link to your task bar LEAD THE FIELD – Earl Nightingale on YouTube

https://youtu.be/7lAvd7_a6K

Think and Grow Rich Full Audio by Napoleon Hill on YouTube

Copy link and add to task bar

https://youtu.be/KgxnR-RyKlI

Its recommended that you listen to these often if not daily for the first 90 days the information in them are gold nuggets just waiting to be plucked.

## The Mind Set

Every day we look at ways to make our life better. This we believe is following what everyone else is doing. We are all the same we are spiritual beings we are made in gods image we have been given the same ability's to think and create our own destiny and desires.

Years pass so quickly, when we are young we are told by people in their 50s and older "Time goes so quick don't waist a minute, enjoy every second we have." Well we laugh and go on with out another thought. People in their late teens 20s 30s and 40s, tend to believe they will live for ever and there is plenty of time. Its once they hit their 50s and 60s they are in the same job for 40 yeas their deep in debt or their life has fully fallen apart, they tend to look back and say what happen,where did that time go? 60 years gone in what seamed like a blink of an eye. You look up one day and you realised there had to be more, and there was, and there still is a lot more,

Its been seen in the (last 10 years) people are waking up to there is more and a good percentage are now exploring that. The concept that this is all there is, is no more. Ignorance and lack of

Education which hasn't been there for you since pre school. When you hear others say life is what you make it, could not ring truer. You own your destiny you start your life in the direction you want to go. To allow others to do that for you would be like letting a 5 year old drive your car, or control you finances.

There is only one captain and that is you, now you can sail blindly through life hoping things will work for you, and no doubt something will, but is that what you have now, is that the life you want for you or for your family? You now have the opportunity to live a life you want to have, the things in life you desire and all you have to do is see it in your mind believe in yourself and its your for the taking.
Have you ever just sat back and thought about all the things you want, about how that thing you desire can change you life or at least better it, nothing is out of your reach. Oh I can hear you saying. No its not I don't have the money. I say don't worry about the Money.

Let me explain. Lets say your dream is to stop renting and own your own home. Yes everyone would love to have their own home and they can, you can. Wait let me finish. If you want a new house go out and get one, its that simple.

I hear the cry's "I don't have the money." As I said you don't need the money, because you haven't made up your mind to get the house yet.

Oh yes you have said I want a house but have you seen it in your mind? Do you know the floor plan of that house? What colour is the bedroom? How big a pool or the back yard? Is it a two car garage for you and your partners car? If you don't have this in your mind your not ready to buy a house.

Let me tell you one of Bobs story this will help you better get were I am going with your house

Bobs calls on a friend and he is offered a coffee as the owner returns to sit in the lounge the owner we will call her May, May says "Do you mind if we sit in the kitchen"? Bob agrees and

they move to the kitchen, its then Bob asked what was wrong with sitting in the living room and May replied "I can not stand that room I hate those curtains" Bob looked at her and said not you don't May if you did they wouldn't be there, you would have changed them. And as long as there up you will never change them. Well May said "I cant take them down I have nothing to replace them. Bob said that is because you have not made the decision to replace then. Bob told her if she keeps them up she has nowhere to put the new curtains as that space is occupied by her old curtains See Bob was trying to explain until you let go of the old, you will never get the new, well May immediately started to take them down. A few weeks later Bob returned to see new curtains hanging in place of the old ones.

Remove the old to allow for the new. The same goes with your house, you want a new house you have to change things. Maybe look at buying things now for your new house. Replace a lamp or table maybe a new bed? Just start making changes, have a burning desire to want a new house. Make a plan work that plan and suddenly you will find that you have manifested the deposit for your new house. Nothing happens with out action.
Write this down on a piece of paper.
I am so great full to be moving into my three bedroom house with a pool and write the date and year. Now put that in your wallet and every day read that out load to yourself and in the time (note do not expect it to happen immediately, allow twelve to eighteen months) Write the year and date you want to be in your new home. Imagine it, write it down read out load every day work your goal. Go buy new rug for one of the rooms what ever will keep you excited about owning and having your own home and tell yourself daily you are thankful for the house tell yourself you already have the home and cement that in your subconscious mind and before you can say "I should have added a spar" you will be in your new home.

This is not free. Nothing in life comes for free, you must set your goal and work towards it. There are those who set a goal and in a year are still in the same position, then they say goal setting doesn't work. It does but you have to take action.

Setting a goal and sitting back waiting for it to happen, it will never happen. Its up to you to work the plan its only then the two shall meet.

When you set a goal you move to a higher vibration. Its a formula. First you have an idea of what you want step 1 then you hold that image in your mind step 2 now this is as far as some people go they think ok I have an idea and I see it in my mind so it must be coming to me.

Well bless their little soles, there are a few more steps, step 3 work the goal this is where you work out when you want it by, lets say you want to go on a cruise in lets say 2 years from today and you know were you want to go or it may be a world cruise great, now you have the idea you see the image in your mind you know were and when you want to go. Now you write it down it doesn't have to be perfect as things happen and you might have to change a few things before the deadline or date. But write it down and put it in you bedroom or bathroom or anywhere you will see it first thing in the morning and last thing at night you can even add cruise liner pictures or island pictures to help keep the image in your mind. Once you have it written down read it aloud every morning when you get up and last thing at night before retiring for the night.

Read it with emotion, emotion will make it real to you conscious mind and it also keeps you excited about your goal.

Your subconscious mind will reject anything that is not delivered with emotion, get excited about it, hey your going on a world cruise you should be excited.

Another thing in the time you are working towards you desired goal go online and study the places you will go to, learn about its history and the people. This will cement the desire deep in your conscious and finally your subconscious. You do this over and over every day and you will find in no time at all you will be booking your world cruise. Now don't worry about the money, if your desire is strong you will find the money will comes in just when your ready to book.

This is working the plan every day give thanks to the universe for your world trip act as if its already booked and be grateful every day by saying "Thank you universe for my wonderful cruise." Act as if its already booked your just waiting for the departure date and you will find your self going from port to port and meeting wonder full people from all cultures and all you had to do is have an idea hold the image in your mind and set the plan. Bon voyage.

"Send me a post card."

## Negative V Positive

Most of us are aware every positive has a negative we can not exist without them. This is why we except the good with the bad, the happy with the sad and the evil and the good and with that north and south pole we have gravity. What goes up must come down. What you put out to the universe is returned from the universe. Couse and Effect vibration and frequency.

We live in an ocean of motion, nothing is ever still.

SandyGallagh explains vibration in the next chapter

Newton's law of gravity https://www.britannica.com/science/gravity-physics/Newtons-law-of-gravity

Newton discovered the relationship between the motion of the Moon and the motion of a body falling freely on Earth. By his dynamical and gravitational theories, he explained Kepler's laws and established the modern quantitative science of gravitation. Newton assumed the existence of an attractive force between all massive bodies, one that does not require bodily contact and that acts at a distance. By invoking his law of inertia (bodies not acted upon by a force move at constant speed in a straight line), Newton concluded that a force exerted by Earth on the Moon is needed to keep it in a circular motion about Earth rather than moving in a straight line. He realised that this force could be, at long range, the same as the force with which Earth pulls objects on its surface downward. When Newton discovered that the acceleration of the Moon is

1/3,600 smaller than the acceleration at the surface of Earth, he related the number 3,600 to the square of the radius of Earth. He calculated that the circular orbital motion of radius R and period T requires a constant inward acceleration A equal to the product of 4π 2nd the ratio of the radius to the square of the time:

## MOTION STATE OF VIBRATION

Motion is constant we are all in a state of vibration although our body seems to look like its still we are in constant vibration.

If you lift your arm out in front of you and hold it still that arm is vibrating. I am not going to give a number but I am sure if you google it you will find the correct answer.

My point is motion, we are always in motion as is the planet that's how we find our emotions sad, happy, d-pressed etc, the vibration we are in at any one time, some call this the swing, hence the word mood swing.
Now this swing can be measured, as is done with pilots to make sure they are on a high swing before they take out an air plain with soles on board. If their on a low swing they are grounded and i am happy to know that.
Everything on the planet is in motion our oceans our rivers out trees, If you see a park bench and you put that under a microscope you would see it vibrating, every thing is in vibration with the planet when you die your still in a flux of vibration if you were not how would your body turn into dust? This brings us back to Negative and positive we could not survive with out the both of them.

# The following article by SandyGallagh will give you a better understanding of the The Law of Vibration

Everything in this Universe, including you, boils down to energy, frequencies, and vibrations.

And within this Universe, there are seven major Universal Laws or Principles that explain how energy, frequencies, and vibrations "work." These laws, which are as real as the law of physics, dictate "the rules to the Game of Life" and how to consciously create the life we want.

Seven Universal Laws at a Glance by SandyGallagh

https://www.proctorgallagherinstitute.com/35331/seven-universal-laws-at-a-glance

### 1. THE LAW OF ATTRACTION OR VIBRATION
To understanding the Law of Attraction, let's first understanding its understanding counterpart, the Law of Vibration.

The Law of Vibration decrees that everything moves, or vibrates, nothing rests. Everything ever created, from the smallest atomic particle to the largest skyscraper, is in a constant state of energetic motion.

Now, the thoughts you think and internalise (get emotionally involved with) are in control of the VIBRATION you're in. As you become conscious of this vibration, you refer to it as how you are "FEELING."

There is a connection between your FEELINGS, what you ATTRACT to yourself, and the RESULTS you get in your life. The vibration, or feeling, you are in leads to the actions you take, and your actions create the results you experience in life.

When you understanding the Law of Attraction, instead of allowing the outside world to dictate what you think and how you feel inside, you start to live from the inside out by choosing and focusing on thoughts that align with what you want. This causes changes in your vibration field to attract or create the results you seek in life.

To see read more on this subject follow the link above by placing it in the search bar.

In the early part of this book I mentioned education and knowledge is key and I know that more than anyone, with leaving school at 15 years old. See I believed Henry Ford invented the first *automobile*. Who invented the first automobile and when?

The German Engineer Karl Benz invented the first motor carriage,

https://www.britannica.com/biography/Karl-Benz

https://www.google.com/search?q=who+invented+the+firat+automobile&rlz=1C1CHBF_en-GBAU905AU907&oq=who+invented+the+firat+automobile&aqs=chrome..69i57j0i13l5j0i13i3 0j0i22i30l3.21969j0j7&sourceid=chrome&ie=UTF-8

See full story Copy link and add to search bar.

Its common that we believe what we are told. My belief was Henry Ford invented the automobile that is false, in fact Mr Ford invented the assembly line in which to build the automobile.

Self education is made so much easier with the use of Google and other internet search engines. Something that we didn't have when I was young.

My first book Out Back Blues, book took me over forty years to complete.

At first I started with pen and paper for the fist 10 years, I almost gave up many times. When I could afford it I purchased my first type writer. I went through a lot of paper and white out, I must tell you.

Then came the first home computer in Australia to be honest I don't even know what I paid for it. I was so excited, well I was not computer illiterate, I must have been on it for eighteen to twenty hours writing my hart out. Also I was unaware that unless its saved (which was not an open with dos) I would lose it. I shut it down and went to bed so happy with the amount of writing I had done with no paper no white out.

The next morning I arose earlier showered and made my coffee, pumped to continue my story, I eagerly headed to the computer switched it on and waited for it to spring to life, after remembering how to get to the page I had written my story on that took me some time but finally I got to the page, it opened and there before me, as the day before when I got to that page was a cursor blinking at me and nothing but an empty page. Well my girlfriend at the time

watched me have a mega tantrum that lasted some hours. It was a year later that I was given a program still not windows but a version of it and finally I could save my work.

I could have given up there and then but my dream my goal was to write my book. If I had of read Think and Grow Rich back then, I can tell you without a shadow of a doubt that it would not have taken me 40 years to complete my book and my life would have gone in a totally different direction.

Its good to be able to sit back now and recall that moment like a movie playing in my head of me acting like a two year old after loosing my story. Now the moral of this story, yes there is a point, that computer may have been unable to store my story in its memory but in my mind it was safe and sound and in 2016, I published Out Back Blues, and two others in the series book 2 Lost in the Out Back and book 3 Real Friends as well as an another self help book Rythem and Melody.

I also have to add that while writing this part of this book I had written 7 pages on day one another 10 pages on day two, by day three I did a massage spell check then continued writing, I was up to page 20 when I looked down and noticed it said page 7, well I didn't have quite the tantrum I had 40 years ago, but it defiantly hurt. It was not, not hitting save that I lost it, it was by hitting save that i lost it. At some stage I went and used the undo option, then when it prompted me to save changes I did, not taking noticed what it had undone till it was to late, great lesson learnt, who said you can't learn stuff at 60?

## Quitters never Win.

## Winners never quit.

Write this out and put it where you can see it and read aloud twice a day once in the morning and once at night.

This helps keep you focused on your goal, its to easily to get distracted and lose sight of your dream. Your mind must stay positive if you neglect this law you will fail to receive all riches you deserve.

Negativity can come from anywhere and anyone. Negative and Positive will be mentioned in later pages.

One of the hardest things is to stop listening to negative people or let them influence your thought keep your mind closed to negative thoughts, keep your goal your dream at the forefront of your mind. By spending time around positive people you have the ability to stop negativity coming into you life. Many look at books for inspiration also with audio books now available you can get positive influences in your life and take that influence on your journey. Keeping negativity out is as simple as stop watching the news, stop listening to the radio, limit your time of multi media outlets. You will soon find your life becoming positive. Suddenly you are associating with positive people and reading positive information. Do what you can to close your mind to all negative influences and watch you life change as you grow. A positive mental attitude is a wonderful and gratifying feeling, you will smile more, be more open to people and they to will feel you being positive and will gravitate to you. Be kind be considerate and most of all be happy and you will stop all negativity coming into your life.

**Don't trade your life for a house or a car or a holiday of your dreams, because that's exactly what you are doing. You are trading your life, to live a better life.**

Bob Proctor.

I know that I have the ability to achieve the object of my definite purpose in life, therefore, I demand of myself persistent, continuous action toward its attainment, and I here and now promise to render such action.

The dominating thoughts of my mind will eventually reproduce themselves in outward physical action and gradually transform themselves into physical reality. Therefore, I will concentrate my thoughts for 30 minutes daily upon the task of thinking of the person that I intend to become. Thereby creating in my mind a clear mental picture.

I know through the theory of autosuggestion, any desire that I persistently hold in my mind will eventually seek some expression through some practical means of obtaining the object or position I desire. I have clearly written down a description of my definite chief aim and I will never stop trying until I develop sufficient self-confidence for it's attainment.

I realise that no wealth or position can long endure unless built upon truth and justice.

I will engage in no transaction that will not benefit all whom it effects.

I will succeed by attracting to myself the forces that I wish to use and the cooperation of other people.

I will induce others to serve me because of my willingness to serve them.

I will eliminate hatred, envy, jealousy, selfishness and cynicism by developing love for all humanity for I know that a negative attitude toward others will never bring me success.

I will cause others to believe in me because I will believe in them and in myself.

I will sign my name to this formula commit to memory and repeat it aloud once a day in full faith that it will gradually influence my thoughts and actions so I will become a self reliant and successful person.

SIGNED: _____

DATE: _____

**Make The Commitment To Yourself**

**Think and Grow Rich**

By printing of and signing this formula you are making a commitment to yourself. Read it aloud once a day.

Bob Proctor was a big believer in repetition by reading or hearing the audible tapes over and over you are cementing the information deep in your subconscious mind. Its believed just ninety days of doing a thing over and over becomes a habit. Before we know it we are in auto mode we do it with out thinking about it.
 With controlling your time on social media checking emails replying to messages and surfing Facebook and Instagram which we spoke about in earlier pages. Its is vital that the habits you are now teaching your subconscious are good habits and habits that guide you to become a better person, become a positive person becomes a happy successful person.

 Having a goal and committing to that goal is life changing and a challenging step,  you are giving up your life to be a better person to accomplish your desires and dreams.

## River People or Goal
Earl Nightingale

Earl Nightingale explains this well. Take the time to listen to this recording.

https://YouTube/TYKPJXRDZfk

Add the link to the search Bar

Goal are an important step to getting what you desire the truth is we all have goals, but very few follow through or know how to, or get disheartened along the way, the destination seems to far away so they give up.

See the list of 6 reasons to set goals. Print this out and read twice daily out aloud and with enthusiasm until you know it off by heart. By doing this you will set deep in your subconscious the 6 rules to goal setting.

List from Think and Grow Rich, by Napoleon Hill

By following these steps and understanding there principles you will find that things in your life are starting to change. But be aware before you start to see the things you desire things can seam like they are heading in the opposite direction. Don't be discouraged, if you stay focused on your goal, you will find things do start to come together. Remember you have the power you just have to believe in yourself.

Education is what pushes you forward, specialised knowledge will help you grow and using your imagination will help you see your goal. Imagination is step 5 of think and grow rich. Go back often and listen to this step and print out the Page supplied. The more you follow these instructions the closer you get to your dream. By knowing your goal and exactly what you want you help bring the plan to life, as stated earlier you control your destiny you have the formula in this book to grow and become successful by understanding that some plans can fail

This is not a reason to quite your plan, go again, you have it in you to be great once you realise that you will succeed. The only on between you and you success is you.

If a plan doesn't work don't scrap it re plan it, maybe it just needs a few tweaks, ask yourself is this plan is obtainable? if you plan is to have a million dollars in your bank by next week then that plan is unobtainable, if its to have 100,000 in two years then work the plan to achieve that goal.

Most of all, believe in yourself. Don't set yourself up to fail by not planing to take action. By taking action you have no choice but to succeed. The positive metal attitude you obtain will lead you to success, work your plan set it in action and you are guaranteed to win.

# Auto Suggestion

1. "Fix in your mind the exact amount of money you desire. It is not sufficient merely to say 'I want plenty of money.' Be definite as to the amount."

There is a psychological reason behind the idea of setting a specific goal. According to **Edwin Locke's studies**, people who set precise and challenging intentions manage to succeed in their plans.

The main reason behind establishing a defined target is that you will better understand the sacrifice and challenging tasks you must make to reach it.

2. "Determine exactly what you intend to give in return for the money you desire. There is no such thing as something for nothing."

The bigger and challenging the goal you have set is, the more you will have to work hard and sacrifice to obtain it. To focus on outstanding achievement and do more than what you usually do, you must take away time and effort from something else.

Will you dedicate to this purpose hours previously committed to fun activities? Moments with friends and family? Your savings? Nothing comes from nothing. You must redirect most, or all, of your effort into the so much desired end to transform the thought into reality.

3. "Establish a definite date when you intend to possess the money you desire."

How long will it take you to reach the craved goal? By choosing a deadline too far away, you might feel that you have a lot of time at your disposal. You might end up procrastinating on every task. At the same time, picking a day too close to the moment of commitment might make you feel anxious and lead to early burnout.

Evaluate carefully the amount of work you must do to accomplish the predetermined purpose and choose wisely the day of your success.

## The Secret of Success

Be consistently candid and honest. Make it a point to speak what's on your mind without fear of judgement. By speaking the truth and being honest, you can support your words with actions that will help you pursue your success. Simply thinking for yourself can make you unforgettable.

**What are the 6 secrets to success?**
6 Secrets of Successful People
1: Don't do it for the $
2: We're not afraid to be outcasts.
3: Work harder than you ever thought possible.
4: understanding failure is good.
5: Be patient, success is a process.
6: Change course when something isn't working.

To be successful you have to know what you want and work towards obtaining it, to sit back and just wish for it or wait for a lucky jackpot or power ball is silly, not to mention expensive. I know people who play lotto every day, whether that be power ball oz lotto or even scratches. Out of all of them the most I heard a friend win is sixteen thousand dollars, but when you do the maths of him playing every week for 40 plus years, he didn't win, he just got some of him money back. And if you look at most lotto winners you will find it does not last, there is a story of a New York bus driver who was broke two weeks after winning a staggering 20 million jackpot. Its true that those who do not understanding the laws of receiving money will not have it for long.

With just hours to go until the $120 million lottery prize is announced for Thursday night, a financial expert has revealed a sobering statistic.

"Most lotto winners actually go broke within a couple of years," Adele Martin, a certified financial planner, said in https://www.news.com.au/national/ive-got-news-for-you/podcast/addc2b261d7ffa5efaf36d1dc52803c0

Its been seen around the world people who get money from windfalls generally spend it all within years of receiving it. Yes you might say they have assets in the house they buy other goods with little to no value or value for that time. Unless they invest it in business and their future growth they will be broke in no time. That is sad but true.

## We Are Creators

We are all gods greatest creation, now it doesn't matter
if you are religious or budhist or athirst, we are all spiritual beings and we are able to create anything we desire.

5% of the 100 become successful.

Through out time we ask why are we here, what is your purposes? We are made in gods image so there for its stands to reason that we are here to create. And we are given the opportunity to achieve that.

All thing are possible we just have to open our minds. You can turn your fantasy into a fact, just look at the past, look around you. Stop reading for one second look up and see everything around you... Everything around you has been created from the mind, some one had seen it in their mind and then created it. And a lot of these people where not educated. some have a few months of schooling. How did they do it with out an education? You will find they hung around with educated people that aligned themselves with confident people they drew from their experiences and knowledge. By submerging yourself around positive people with the know how and education and a positive mental attitude, you will find you can do and create anything. The only thing stopping you is you.

Open your wonderful mind and dream see what you can create who knows you may change the world, at least you will change your world just believe in you.

What you have to do is stop letting others tell you your not able to do it, its up to you to push past that fear barrier and allow yourself to dream. Unfortunately we listen to others who tell us we cant do it or were crazy. That is a good thing, if you stop and listen to other people it means they are not thinking they are court up in their little world and they lack the power of understanding they can change their life, unfortunately they are conditioned to one way the TV the media ram this home every day, we see images on the tube and told this is how we have to live, if people are walking towards a cliff with their eyes shut are you going to follow them. If a group of people are all heading in one direction and you see one person heading the opposite direction follow that person because you can guarantee that person is thinking's is dreaming has a goal and a plan, hes not just following the masses controlled by the media.

Think big! This is not a time to think small or put limits on yourself. Where will you be in three years? What do you want your life to look like by then? Your Future Self is your guide for where you are going, for what you're going to do, what is going to show up, and who you are going to become. The possibilities are endless. It's your life you control your destiny.

You control your destiny you control your desires.

Are you looking for Your Daily Future Self to be emailed straight to your inbox? Looking for more directions on how to fill out Your Daily Future Self? Keep reading! This tool can help accelerate your growth and bring positively into your mindset.

**Cabin in the woods of Vermont with enough land for ATVs?** Check. Beautiful, healthy third child? Check. Build, own, and hold an office building as an asset? Check. These are all things I wrote down on my

Future Self worksheet over three years ago that came to fruition in the past couple of years. Your Future Self is one of the most impact tools that I've ever used to make my dreams for the future a reality. You can too. One of the coolest things about Your Future Self is that it gets you to think differently and be purposeful about your goals. Your Future Self is your North Star, your navigation, that will bring your dreams into clear focus so that you are not simply floating through life with no paddle, and no direction.

**HERGENROTHER** https://adamhergenrother.com/creating-your-future-self-today/

Add the link to your search Bar to see full story on Adam Hergenrother.

There are a few best practices to keep in mind as you are creating Your Future Self:

1. Think about what you want your life to look like in three years....
2. Write your vision out in the present tense, as if you have already accomplished those goals three years from now.
3. Make sure you are using very specific, measurable goals.

# Time is Ticking

The older we get the wiser we get unfortunately its when we watch our lives fleeting by that we realise we missed it. one minute we are a pimpled face teenager with no idea were we are headed. Oh don't get me wrong some people at the earlier age of 6 or 7 now what they want, some achieve their goals, a majority don't. So here we are a teenager at school trying to work out what and were we want to be in ten years.

Do a survey at your school and ask the kids were do they see themselves in 10 years. Out of 100 people 2% will have a clear goal of their future. 5% will say they think they know and the remaining 93% will say they have no idea.

Time can be a good thing as long as you have a goal, it took me a long time to learn this and understanding that a goal gives your life a purpose a direction a reason to get up out of bed everyday.

**There are a few best practices to keep in mind as you are creating Your Future**

1. Think about what you want your life to look like in three years....
2. Write your vision out in the present tense, as if you have already accomplished those goals three years from now.
3. Make sure you are using very specific, measurable goals.
4. Evert thing we do are from goal setting although were not aware of it, to go shopping you have set a goal, to take the kids to the beach you have set a goal, to take a partner out for dinner you have set a goal.. What is a goal?

   The Dictionary tells us

   1. (in soccer, rugby, hockey, and some other games) a pair of posts linked by a crossbar and typically with a net between, forming a space into or over which the ball has to be sent in order to score.

   2. the object of a person's ambition or effort; an aim or desired result. "he achieved his goal of becoming King of England"

## HISTORICAL USAGE OF GOAL

Goal has no reliable etymology. It appears for the first and only time in Middle English as *gol* "boundary, limit" in the mid-14th century. Some authorities suggest that *gol* was a borrowing from Middle French *gaule, waulle* "pole, stick," from an unattested Germanic cognate of Old Frisian *waal, walu* "rod," which is of no real help. The second recorded occurrence of goal, then spelled *gole,* is in the first half of the 16th century, with the meaning "finishing point of a race, finish line." The extended sense "aim or purpose, outcome of effort or ambition" also dates from the first half of the 16th century. By the late 16th century, goal, at this point spelled *goale,* had also acquired the meaning, now obsolete, "starting point of a race," a translation of one of the many meanings of Latin *finis* (which also meant "boundary, limit" and "finishing point of a race, finish line"). To achieve your goal.

## Now We ask why is setting a goal so important

What is the importance of setting a goal?

Setting goals helps trigger new behaviours, helps guides your focus and helps you sustain that momentum in life. Goals also help align your focus and promote a sense of self-mastery. In the end, you can't manage what you don't measure and you can't improve upon something that you don't properly manage. To not set a goal will leave you wondering around with no erection in life. No real purpose. You will find in this book goal setting is mentioned a lot there is a reason for that, from the dawn of man we have been setting goal if we didn't we would be extinct or still in the caves.

Our entire purpose is a goal, a goal to learn a goal to create a goal to survive. Very thing we have around us comes from someone setting a goal. You set goal to better your life to give it purpose when you go to bed you set your alarm to get up to go to work, that's a goal, yes its a habit and subconsciously you do it every day but its still a goal, you set for yourself, now whether you get up in the morning and go to work or not makes no difference, your goal was achieved by setting your alarm. The rest is if you follow the rest of that goal by putting it into action and getting up to go to work. See a goal with out action is not a goal, its an idea a thought, Lets say you set the alarm for 6am there is your goal, you achieved that part of the goal, you thought about it and put that into action. That is the law in goal setting. Never leave the place where you set a goal without taking some action toward it. This prevents the number one goal procrastination, from setting in and creates momentum toward your goal.

What is the law of polarity?

The law of polarity is the principle that everything has two "poles": good and evil, love and hate, attraction and disconnection. Think of the North and South Poles on a globe or a battery with its negative and positive terminals. Everything in the universe has an opposite.

Like Ying and Yang you cant have one with out the other, cause and effect, when you set that alarm you set that in motion to sleep to awake to stay in bed or get up every action has a reaction. As night is followed by day. No goal can be achieved if its not followed up by action. You set the alarm to get up at 6am, at 6 the alarm goes of you hit snooze or ignore it, you haven't taken action to your goal of getting up. No action no goal, although you did start your goal by setting the alarm. My point being if you set a goal you can only achieve or reach that goal by action. Its like you want to lose weight so you say ill get up at 6am and ill go to the gym. At 6 you wake up and you go back to sleep you are not going to lose weight because you didn't take action. It all starts with attitude is you have a good positive attitude you can do anything, set goal after goal and achieve them over and over again. Unfortunately when people talk about goals they don't tell you that it takes work and commitment to achieve the goal, this is why many fail. They are not prepared to do the work. Lets take the scenario of losing wright, you get out of bed you go to the gym do your 1 hour workout. that night you set your alarm at 6 to wake up to hit the gym the next day. the alarm goes off now your body is going through changes from the workout the day before, you are in pain and you say nope to hard and you go back to sleep. Many of you can relate. So whats the solution then?

The solution is quite easy, see you set your goal to work out for 1 hour your body is now getting a shock from the exercising and you are feeling the affect's that are uncomfortable. Many will say you have to put up with it push through the pain. I say if that works for them good for them, but what you need to do is change your goal Lets say you want to lose 20 kilos and your goal is 1 hour a day 6 days a week. What you need to do is change that goal to smaller chunks, lets say lose 5 kilos to start with and instead of 1 hour a day, do 10 or 15 minutes a day, gradually let your body adjust to the changes it will have from weights or crunches. Small bits per day will help as it gets easier, each day or week increase it by 10 minutes. You will find within a few months you are doing 1 hour a day and you are getting closer to the goal of losing that 20 kilos,. Just because you set a goal does not mean you can not adjust it to get the desired end result. Goal setting doesn't have to be hard work, it just takes you to use your mind and think how you can best achieve your goals.

Any steady rule when goal setting would be just focus on one goal at a time, avoid getting overwhelmed. experience the success of achieving a goal, build momentum for the next goal. People tend to try and set multiple goal and when one fails (General through lack of planning) they give up on all the goals. Pick one goal and see it through till its completion. Remember you setting a goal not multitasking.

# The journey towards reaching your goal

"What you get by achieving your goals is not as important as what you become by achieving your goals." — Zig Ziglar

1. Don't Be Fixed On The Destination:

When you focus on the destination alone, you forgo the good things that take place in-between.

You are wired to thrive. It is formed into your DNA to rise above your perceived limitations.

I know it may not seem that way. Instead of being resentful of not reaching your destination, enjoy the process of working towards your goals.

Before long, conditions will turn out better than expected if you shift your attention away from the outcome every once in a while.

Author Jeff Olson states in *The Slight Edge: Secret to a Successful Life:* "Here is the amazing thing — and I've seen this happen so many times, yet it never ceases to fill me with awe: when you set your goals, life has a way of rearranging itself, a series of events starts in motion that you could never have predicted or planned, to get you there."

2. Take Your Eyes Off The Prize:

Have you ever set a goal to lose weight with a fixed number of how much you intended to lose?

Recall how you chose this figure?

I'm certain you applied little logic other than knowing that it felt right.

What if you re framed the goal to become healthy instead?

Would that place you in a better position to achieve your goal?

You will be surprised to not only lose weight, but your health improves by clearing up issues that plagued you for years.

There is a better way of achieving goals other than the usual methods espoused. The key is not being fixed on a particular result, but **allowing the process to unfold in due course**.

Sadly, less than 10% of people reach their goals because excuses and life impedes attaining them. The message is simple,re frame **your goals to become process orientated.**

Author Larry Weidel states in, *Serial Winner: 5 Actions to Create Your Cycle of Success:* "I have watched so many people work so hard for a goal, putting in tremendous amounts of blood, sweat, and tears. And then, for one reason or another, they get overwhelmed and quit. The big disaster is that their personal investment is washed away and they never receive the benefit of all their hard work."

3. Enjoy The Process:

I attended a money management workshop some time ago with valuable insights. The presenter proposed we spend money buying experiences instead of material objects.

He reasoned, experiences leave an indelible mark on us and contribute to our long term happiness.

They add to the rich tapestry of life as distinct to buying material objects. YouTube blogger Casey Neistat makes a point of devoting an entire episode to this principle in a video titled: What's Most Important.

Applying this rule to goals, buy the process instead of the destination.

**Buy rewarding life experiences that support your goals**, instead of being fixed on the result.

A virtue of success is an inherent curiosity. It is a child-like fascination of your mind's natural ability to find answers to questions.

B

F

o

y to notice.

ons-why-the-journey-

Evolution of computers This makes it seem as if computers are superior, but the truth is **the human brain is much more advanced and efficient and has more raw computing power than the most impressive supercomputers ever built**

Evolution of computers This makes it seem as if computers are superior, but the truth is **the human brain is much more advanced and efficient and has more raw computing power than the most impressive supercomputers ever built**..

#

## I HAD A DREAM

What was Malcolm's dream?

He had a dream of **justice and self-determination for his people that was free of violence, with ideals and principles**. He dreamed of equal access to education, tolerance, consensus-building, and, above all, fairness. Malcolm X was born Malcolm Little on May 19, 1925 in Omaha, Nebraska.

It took but one man to have a dream and share that dream with the world. A dream that changed the world a dream that seamed so impossible yet when put in to action changed the course of history in 1925.Whats your dream? could you be the next Thomas Edison, Henry Ford or Malcolm X? Your mind is so powerful, you can not comprehend its full potential, most humans use just 10% of their brain and scientist have proved the brain has more computing power than a super computer?

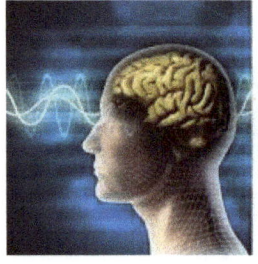 

The human brain is more energy-efficient than computers. Our 10 billion neurons only use 10 watts – that's 10x more efficient tha. That explains why you can still read a book even if you're very tired You have the capacity to store and delete information to your mind and like a conventional computer you can store information and retrieve on request you have the ability to bring up memory and pictures in your mind and the ability to hold that memory physically in your hand. You are a walking talking human create all you have t do is see it in your mind to turn that image into an idea, set a goal for that idea, put that goal into action and truly believe you will achieve that goal and before you know it you have manifested that goal, You are now living that dream, you are now holding that image in your hand.

# MANIFEST YOUR DREAM

When is the last time you manifested your dream?

The Art Of Manifestation

The first step of using the law of attraction to manifest your dreams is challenging the scarcity mindset and

Shifting to a more positive way of thinking—but you can't stop there! After all, the law of attraction is not a magic wand. We all have layers of limiting beliefs, fears, and blocks that cannot be changed overnight. Instead, in order to become a master at manifesting using the law of attraction, we have to put in the work of undoing the negative patterns that have been stored in our unconscious and replacing them with more empowering ones.

It's not easy, but here are nine helpful habits you can implement right now to start using the law of attraction to manifest your dreams:

1. Note what you focus on.
Start by noting what you instinctively focus on. Do you usually pay attention to what's going right in life, or what's going wrong? When you're working on manifesting your dreams, obstacles and challenges will inevitably arise. But when you focus on what's right, you become more of a problem-solver and can move through these obstacles with more ease.

2. Keep a worry list.
Since the brain has a negativity bias, it's no surprise that people are inclined to worry all the time. In order to kick the habit, try keeping a "worry list" for two weeks where you write down worries the second they come to you. This practice will not only help release the heavy energy that often keeps us stuck, but it will also help you review your worries after the fact to see if any of them were actually warranted or not. Your brain will then have proof that worrying is often a waste of energy.

3. Practice diaphragmatic breathing.
The Ultimate Guide To Breath work

Practice this breathing technique for instant stress relief & calm. Take the class now.
Breathing from your belly, not your chest, spend a few minutes making your exhales longer than your inhales. If your inhale is 6 counts, make your exhale 8 counts, for example. This type of breathing activates

the parasympathetic nervous system, which is responsible for our rest-and-digest response. It will help produce a sense of relaxation and contentment and allow you to approach life with a clearer head.

4. Quiet the monkey mind with meditation.
Meditation quiets the monkey mind, which is naturally biased toward negativity. Remember: Meditating will NOT stop your thoughts, but it will show you how fleeting they are. Therefore, it can help you withdraw attention from stressful, negative patterns that your mind has created over time.

5. Move your body in whatever way feels good to you.
Negative emotions get stored in our bodies on a cellular level. Moving is one way to release stress and negative energy. It doesn't have to be intense; you can dance, practice yoga, or go for a walk.

6. Keep a gratitude journal.
Gratitude is one of the simplest ways to raise your positive vibrations. When we recognise our great fortune and appreciate all our blessings, it automatically puts us into a "feel-good" energetic vibration.

7. Write down your goals and connect to your "why."
Writing down a list of your goals will help you get clear and take more inspired action. Be sure that when you do, you connect to your

8. Visualise what it will look like when you achieve your dreams.
Once you've written down your goals and connected with your why, read from the list first thing in the morning and right before bed every day. Take a few minutes to visualise and connect with the feeling of achieving your dreams.

9. Feel like you already have what you want.
Feeling is believing. Let these visualisations transport you to a world in which everything has gone your way. Pay attention to the details: What this world looks like, feels like, and sounds like. Doing so will help generate more excitement and positive attitude it will encourage you to continue taking inspired action towards your dreams.

Whether or not you subscribe to the law of attraction principles, at the very least implementing these habits can help you get clear on exactly what you want—and they might just help you get it, too.

Klaus Vedfelt https://www.oprahdaily.com/life/a30244004/how-to-manifest-anything/
You may be familiar with manifestation, or the laws of attraction. After all, the process was the focus of a 2006 bestselling book, The Secret, which sold more than 30 million copies—and it's something that thought leaders, including Deepak Chopra, Eckhart Tolle, Gabrielle Bernstein, Iyanla Vanzant, and Oprah, have spoken about. (For the record, they all agree that you really can manifest things.)

But, first things first: Even though manifesting is about turning your dreams into reality, it does require that you to take proactive steps toward whatever it is you desire—so you shouldn't expect it to happen instantly or overnight while you sleep. That said, it's a small price to pay (at least in our humble opinion) for something that can have such a profound impact on your life:

"You control a lot by your thoughts, and we control a lot by our joined thoughts...by what I [and we] believe," Oprah told LinkedIn CEO Jeff Weiner in 2015. "When I started to figure that out for myself, I became careful of what I think and what I ask for," she explained. "I was like, What else can I do? What else can I manifest? Because I have seen it work. I have seen it happen over and over again.

## ABOUT THE BOOK https://gabbybernstein.com/universe-has-your-back/

Each story and lesson in this book guides you to release the blocks to what you long for most: happiness, security and clear direction.

Learn how to let go of the need to control so you can relax into a sense of certainty and freedom. Making the shift from fear to faith will give you a sense of power in a world that all too often makes us feel utterly powerless.

Follow the secrets revealed in this book to unleash the presence of your power and know always that the Universe has your back.

Your energetic shift clears space for more miracles on a global scale. Not only will you experience massive abundance — you'll help heal the world, too

## THANK THE UNIVERSE

Thanking the universe for your abundance
Every Day when I wake up I do my mediation read out load my goals and desires then I spend a few minutes thanking the universe for everything she offers me. Yes she after all it is mother nature. I thank her for my life my health by love for others my abundance of wealth and my happiness, by thanking the universe every day I am offering something to the universe, my gratitude and what you give, you get back in abundance. So spend a few minutes, night and morning thanking the universe and you will find inner peace love and harmony towards all humanity, plant life and animals big or small.

Burning Desire

I immediately am reminded of the great worrier that Napoleon Hill mentioned in his book Think and Grow Rich

A long while ago, a great warrior faced a situation which made it necessary for him to make a decision which insured his success on the battlefield. He was about to send his armies against a powerful foe, whose men outnumbered his own. He loaded his soldiers into boats, sailed to the enemy's country, unloaded soldiers and equipment, then gave the order to burn the ships that had carried them. Addressing his men before the first battle, he said, "You see the boats going up in smoke. That means that we cannot leave these shores alive unless we win! We now have no choice--we win--or we perish! They won.

To have no retreat means only one option to forge ahead, knowing you have to achieve your goal. For many of the rags to riches story you read on line (Not the Gurus trying to flees you of your coin) more the person who lost everything was at rock bottom and thought their life was over, that was the hand that they were dealt. Then one day either a dream a feeling, an intuition or something they were watching or someone they may have been talking to hit that part of the mind that said you can change if you believe in you self. I know this from my own story going back to the mid 90s I was broke unemployed lived in a three bedroom

flat had friend (Loosely translated) we drank smoked cones (Marijuana) all night then slept all day and we did that for three solid months. We didn't live we just existed contributing nothing to society.

Well one afternoon I awoke after spending the night doing the same thing as we had been doing for the past three months, but this day I didn't wake up go down stares stepping between the multiple sleeping body's on the floor. No I woke up I sat on the end of my bed and My mind asked me a question "What are you doing"? Well I sat there rubbing my eyes and I answered "I don't know" and I truly didn't know, at that moment I said out load "No more" At that moment I got up, showered got dressed, i then told my mate speedy "Pack you bags were getting out of this shit hole." One of the sleeping body's over heard the conversation and said, "You cant Just leave." I looked at her and with full passion and belief in myself I said, "We can and we are." And we did, we drove down south where we camped in a tent that we purchased with an unemployment check I received days before, we started a new chapter of our lives. See there was no way we where ever going to change unless I took action and we went on a journey, a journey that taught me anything is possible if you set a goal and you have a burning desire. I burnt my bridge I couldn't go back I had no choice but to go forward as the warrior said "We win or we perish. I won. I changed my life and all it took was to listen to my inner self that asked "What are you doing"? Next time you hear you inner voice listen to it, it has an important message.

## In Conclusion

the topics in this book are just general guides that have worked for countless people and I am saying, if you follow the steps the research in this books and YouTube videos that I have given you links to, if you believe in yourself then there is no reason these theory's and practices can not work for you.

The only person who can change you is you, whether you are hi five-ing yourself in the mirror or listening to the audio books over and over again and writing down your goals or even starting to set goals and take action. And if this is working for you its because you have that willingness to change. Change can come in small steps. stop hitting the snooze button to get an extra 15 minutes sleep. When you wake up at 5 or 6am get up put your feed on the floor, make your bed the minute you get up so you don't go and crawl back into it. Shower and do your 15 minute meditation, read your goals aloud then thank the universe for what ever your thank full for.

Bob Proctor suggests making a list of 6 goal every night, not big ones just goals that will help you structure your day. If you don't get them done that day that's fine just work through the list till completed.

https://youtu.be/Gzj7zP5BXdc
Watch the video carefully to learn the habit you MUST develop. Do YOU have this skill?

Follow all the steps we have laid out for you, watch the videos and follow the advise and before you know it you will be looking back at the burning bridge behind you heading for you success and you will be part c that 5% that make it to the a life of independent wealth.

It does not matter your age you can reach your goal at 60 any goal is achievable if you follow it up and take action.

1. Repetition is the way to learn and grow.
2. Tell yourself every day you are capable of doing anything you set your mind to.
3. put your goal in to action.
4. Keep a positive mental attitude when you read your goals out aloud use enthusiasm.
5, Act as if you have already achieved tour goal.
6. Have that winning image, become the person you want to be.
7, Be prepared for success its coming.
8. Look in the mirror an us the I an. Example; I Am Successful I am Loved I am financially independent.
9. Desire it and you will receive it.
10. Believe in your self make the changes to be the best you.
11. Stop listening to negative people.
12 never stop setting goals.

I hope this self help book was helpful in some way to let you see that you are already great you are already successful you can be who and what ever you want at any age I know "60 years gone" and i am still going strong.

At the beginning of this book I shared a story of the two shoe salesmen who were sent to Tanzania to sell shoes, well both of those men became very wealth and now in Tanzania in South Africa everyone wears shoes.
Keep a positive mental attitude and there will be no stopping you.